Spilling the Beans on...

William Shakespeare

and other Elizabethans
from around the Globe

First published in 2000 by Miles Kelly Publishing,
Bardfield Centre, Great Bardfield, Essex CM7 4SL

Printed in China

ISBN 978-1-902947-21-1

4 6 8 10 9 7 5

Cover design and illustration: Inc
Layout design: GQ
Art Direction: Clare Sleven

:Spilling the Beans on...

William Shakespeare

and other Elizabethans
from around the Globe

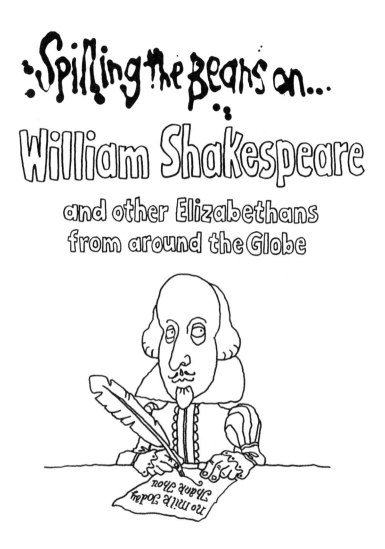

No mile Today
Shank Thou

by Dennis Hamley

Illustrations   Mike Mosedale

About the Author

Dennis Hamley lives in Hertford with his wife and two cats. He has a son who is a scientist, a daughter in publishing and a grandson.

He has written many children's books. *The War and Freddy* was shortlisted for the Smarties Prize. He writes mysteries for a children's crime series, including *Death Penalty* and *Deadly Music*, and is now writing six mysteries set in the Middle Ages. He also writes football, ghost, animal and railway stories.

He often visits schools for talks and he also runs creative writing courses.

Contents

He Makes Me Sick

Rewind 400 years. Stop. Now go a little further back even than that.

Stop.

It's 1592.

Queen Elizabeth the First is ruling England and Wales. James the Sixth rules Scotland.

The Spanish Armada has been seen off. England is best. At least, the English say so.

London is where it all happens. And in a bedroom overlooking the noisy streets along the River Thames, a man lies in bed.

His name is Robert Greene. He is dying. And that's not the only reason he's not happy.

He calls for pen, ink and paper. He must write down what he thinks while he still can. He's got to get this off his chest.

He chews his quill pen as he ponders:
What do I want to say. What, precisely, is my gripe?

All I ever wanted to do was write plays. I've done a few and they aren't bad. Well, I don't think so, anyway. I reckon my *Friar Bacon and Friar Bungay* was a real cracker.

All right, I know others are better. My mate Tom Kyd's for one. That *Spanish Tragedy* of his would scare you half to

death. And what about Kit Marlowe? His *Dr Faustus* really makes audiences shiver. Yes, those plays are about as good as you can get. Tom and Kit know what they're doing.

But what have we got now? Ignorant little twerps come along thinking they can do it all, thinking it's EASY. There's one in particular. Who does he think he is? Where has he come from?

Robert has made himself so angry that he's bitten the pen too hard and his teeth meet through the quill.

He's turned up in London from some place in the country nobody's heard of. He's only an actor. He's not one of us *real* playwrights. We ignore him.

He's had no proper education. He can't recite Latin and Greek until his ears fall off, like proper playwrights do. So he's *thick*.

There's a lot of rumours about him. Some say he's on the run because he poached some rich bloke's deer. So he's a *thief.*

Some say he's got a wife and kids back home and he's run away from them. So he's a *rat.*

Some say he's been in hiding because he's a secret Catholic. That really is serious. We should turn him in to the authorities. He could be spying for the Spaniards. Or worse. *The Pope.*

BUT NOBODY REALLY KNOWS.

Robert Greene pauses again. He still hasn't written a word.

I don't really care either, he thinks. As long as he doesn't write any more of those rotten, boring plays. People like him get the theatre a bad name. I mean, look at them.

What about his comedies? There's that *Two Clowns* – sorry, *Gentlemen of Verona*. Funny? I've read shopping lists I've laughed at more.

Can he write tragedies? Not if *Titus Andronicus* is anything to go by. I mean, nobody likes a bit of blood on the stage more than me, but, well – these disgusting brothers cutting a young girl's tongue out on stage, then her father cutting his own hand off, then baking the brothers in a pie and serving it up to their mother? *And she eats it.* Over the top or what?

All right, histories. I've never been so bored as I was with *Henry VI*. But as soon as it was finished, I found that was only the first part . So I sat through the second and that was *worse*.

"I don't believe it," I said. Well, I had to, because HE DID A THIRD. If you don't know when to stop, you're no good at plays, that's what I say.

Oh. dear! In his anger Robert has chewed off the end of his quill pen. He spits bits of feather over the bedclothes, dips what's left of the pen in the inkpot and starts writing.

How shall he put this? If it's too obvious he might make trouble for himself, but he needs to warn Tom and Kit and the rest to watch out.

He'll be devious.
Ah, he's got it. He starts to write.

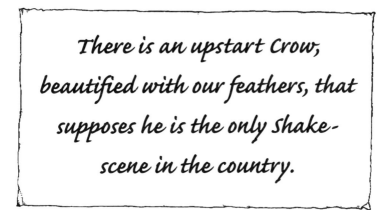

There is an upstart Crow, beautified with our feathers, that supposes he is the only Shake-scene in the country.

11

Is that clear enough? Is it strong enough? He chews his pen again, then speaks aloud.

"That Shakspere. He makes me SICK!"

He's tired. Time for a sleep. He'll finish the rest later.

As he closes his eyes, he remembers one of the first plays he ever saw. He sighs. "Ah, *Gorboduc.* They don't write them like that any more."

Well, he's asked the question. *Who was Shakespeare?* But then, you might ask, *Who was Robert Greene?* I'll tell you later. All in good time.

Is this how it was?

We don't know much more now about Shakespeare than
Greene did then. There were no computer programs
to follow every detail of a person's life.
Shakespeare was only born an
ordinary boy in a tiny
English town, so
who'd bother
noticing anyway?
What there is has
to be put together
and made into a
pattern like a jigsaw.

So we can start with **definites** and **could be's.**

First definite

William Shakespeare was christened in Stratford-on-Avon on April 26th, 1564. Stratford was a sleepy town in the midlands, hardly bigger then than a village is now.

First could be

Was he really born on April 23rd? It's a strange coincidence that it's also St George's Day. (Though not a bit surprising that it's World Book Day as well.)

Second definite

His father was John Shakespeare, who made gloves and was a town councillor. John married Mary Arden. They had nine children. William was the third, but he was their first son.

Second could be

There was a grammar school in Stratford where boys could learn Latin and Greek, because that's what they needed to get on in life then. Girls didn't need to get on in life, so they learnt nothing. William probably went there, but not for long. His parents took him away because he needed to earn money to help the family. Every year the Shakespeares went to Coventry to watch the Miracle Plays. William never forgot them.

Third could be

Years later, after Shakespeare was dead, the son of an actor-friend of his told a story that as a boy William once worked in a butcher's shop and *"When he killed a calf, he would do it in a high style and make a speech."*

They did things differently then. Is this true? Who knows. This actor was known to be a bit of a joker.

After that – *nothing.* Until:

Third definite

In November 1582, a special licence was issued for William Shakespeare to marry Anne Hathaway.

Fourth definite

Their daughter Susanna was christened in the parish church

in May 1583. Work it out for yourself. According to her tombstone, Anne was eight years older than William. So when they married, he was eighteen and she was twenty-six.

Fourth could be

He stole Sir Thomas Lucy's deer and had to get out quick. Where best to go but London? What best for him to do but be an actor?

Fifth could be

After his next child was born, a boy called Hamnett, poor Will decided he'd had enough. So what best but to run away to London and be an actor?

Sixth could be

But perhaps he didn't just run away from the family. Perhaps he went because doing something he was good at was the best way of making money. He sent money back to Stratford and often stayed there. In the end he went back to live. He bought New Place, the best house in the town. Sadly, it was pulled down in 1759 just to annoy people, by a theatre-hating clergyman. William planted a mulberry tree in the garden and this clergyman cut that down as well.

Seventh could be

William went away to be "a scholemaster in the countrey".

Where? Why not Hoghton Hall in Lancashire, as tutor to children of a rich man called Alexander de Hoghton?

They still believe it there, anyway.

Eighth could be

The Shakespeare family were secret Catholics. Round about this time, things got even rougher than usual for Catholics and, for fear of being found out, the Shakespeares went far away and hid.

- **Where did they hide?**

Perhaps it was in Lancashire, in Hoghton Hall, where they were all secret Catholics.

- **Is it true?**

I haven't a clue.

Definitely the last definite (for now)

In 1592, Robert Greene wrote nasty things about Shakespeare, the London actor and playwright.

This means that, some time after 1583 but well before 1592, Shakespeare came to London.

What happened next?

What did Shakespeare do when he got to London?

One of five things could have happened. They are set out below. You must decide for yourselves. I won't give you any clues.

Did he:

a) Find nowhere to live and no job either, so he slept in a cardboard box in a shop doorway?

b) Go to Highbury and ask for a trial with Arsenal?

c) Turn up in Paddington Green police station and end up on trial whether he asked to or not?

d) REALISE HE DIDN'T LIKE LONDON AFTER ALL SO WENT BACK TO STRATFORD-ON-AVON AND WAS NEVER HEARD OF AGAIN?

e) Join a theatre company?

Right. Have you decided?

Is it a)?

Unlikely. Cardboard hadn't been invented yet.

Is it b)?

Unlikely. There is no record of a William Shakespeare ever having a trial with Arsenal – or Spurs, Chelsea or West Ham. Or even Wimbledon. However, much, much later Shakespeare did play for Walsall, but they were only in the third division then.

THIS IS TRUE. You'll know how later.

Is it c)?

Impossible to say. Police records were very poor then. This was because there were no police.

Is it d)?

Unlikely. If it was, I wouldn't be writing this book. Although some people would say it is true because they won't believe

Shakespeare wrote the plays. In fact they think *anyone* but Shakespeare wrote them. They think a man called Bacon did. He was no relation to Greene's *Friar Bacon*. He was nothing to do with *Hamlet*, either.

Is it e)?
NOT NECESSARILY.

Yes, we know he ended up in an acting company. But did he join when he got to London or was he in it before? He could have joined when he was still in Stratford. Actors used to tour all round the country, doing their plays in inn-yards. Perhaps Shakespeare went one night. Could this be how it happened?

ACT 1, SCENE 1.
THE COURTYARD OF AN INN

The galleries and the yard itself are crowded. A colourful figure appears. He is a herald and blows a fanfare on a trumpet.

HERALD
Tonight we give you the stirring play by our
esteemed friend Master Robert Greene,
The Honourable History of Friar Bacon and
Friar Bungay!

ENTER THE PROLOGUE
The audience is hushed and rapt. A member of the audience whispers to the person next to him.

SHAKESPEARE *(for it is he)*
This magic scene has opened up to show
A mirror of the world to any who
Will let their hearts and minds and eyes roam free
And soak themselves in all the riches here.

PERSON NEXT TO HIM

Are you all right, mate? You want to watch it.

ACT 1, SCENE 2
THE SAME

Friar Bacon and Friar Bungay is over.
Audience cheers, claps and puts money in box on way out.
Shakespeare has remained. He sees the leading actor
and goes to him.

SHAKESPEARE

Excuse me sir,
may I join your
company?

LEADING
ACTOR

Why, my likely
feller-me-lad, we
could do with a
fine, sprightly
young jackanapes
like yourself.

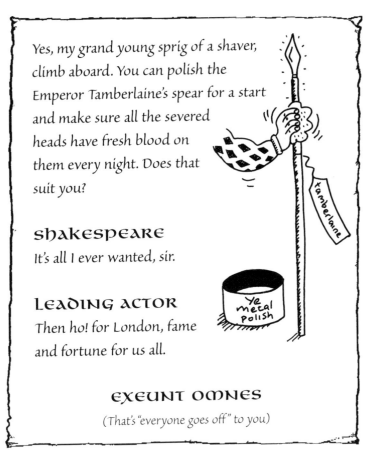

Yes, my grand young sprig of a shaver, climb aboard. You can polish the Emperor Tamberlaine's spear for a start and make sure all the severed heads have fresh blood on them every night. Does that suit you?

SHAKESPEARE
It's all I ever wanted, sir.

LEADING ACTOR
Then ho! for London, fame and fortune for us all.

EXEUNT OMNES

(That's "everyone goes off" to you)

Well, it might have been. On the other hand, let's have a different second scene.

ACT 1, SCENE 2

Friar Bacon and Friar Bungay ends. Audience shouts, cheers and claps wildly. Puts even more money in box on way out.

shakespeare
I don't believe it.

person next to him.
I know. Wasn't it brilliant?

shakespeare
Brilliant? That? An awful mess, a joke,
With empty words and vain emotions, quite
Breathtaking in its whole stupidity.

Shakespeare leaves audience and runs on to stage, where he buttonholes leading actor.

leading actor
Why, my fine young
feller-me-lad, we could
do with a sprightly -

shakespeare
Enough of that.

What means this froth and pother
That dares to show itself upon our stage,
Such sound and fury signifying naught
But vanity and hollow vacancy?

LEADING ACTOR
Oh. So you think you could do better, do you?

SHAKESPEARE
Sirrah, I could. I'd write you such a play
To make the seat and centre point
Of all your feelings shake and sigh and shout
With ecstasy and wild abandonment,
Would freeze your -

LEADING
ACTOR
All right, I get
the point. I
want a
two hour
play about
King Henry VI

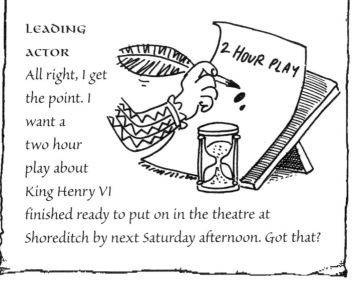

finished ready to put on in the theatre at
Shoreditch by next Saturday afternoon. Got that?

shakespeare

Indeed I have. I'll write you such a play
To make the rafters ring with cries of joy
And be the first of many that will bring
The whole of England to your theatre fine.

Leading actor

Well, as long as you know. Then ho! for London,
fame and fortune for us all.

exeunt omnes

Or he might have been in London already...

The big world outside

Now William's on his way to London, what will he find outside Stratford?

A very strange place indeed. England was changing fast.

How?

For hundreds of years things were settled. People knew their place. Peasants were at the bottom, then tradesmen, then knights, then barons. Then came the king. After him was the Pope. Then it was angels and archangels all the way up to God. God made it that way. Binding everything together was the Church. Until now.

Why now?

Two hundred years before, Barons started rebelling against

their kings, putting them off their thrones and putting other barons on. There were civil wars like the Wars of the Roses about who should be king. There were peasants' revolts.

The Bible was put into English and other languages, not just Latin.

Printing was invented. More people could read – more had books. They began thinking. TERRIBLE. You could be burnt at the stake for that. But perhaps the world was round, perhaps it moved round the Sun and not the Sun round it – perhaps, perhaps, perhaps...

Starting in Italy and spreading through Europe, artists made pictures and statues, wrote poems, and music for their beauty and meaning, not just to praise God.

Yes, the world was on the move.

What happened next?

Henry VIII, Elizabeth's father, became seriously fed up with Catherine of Aragon, his first wife. He asked the Pope for a divorce. The Pope said "No!" very loudly. Henry said, "Then tough. I'll have my own Church." So started the Church of England. Henry got rid of all the monasteries and took their land and riches. Now he was Head of the Church.

But heaven help anybody who didn't join it. Now the beheadings and burnings started. Henry didn't start his new Church so people could think for themselves. Catholics who didn't change were called "Recusants". They hid. Their priests, if they were caught, were hanged or beheaded.

Henry did a lot of that, did he?
He did, to keep the Catholics quiet.

But Henry forgot – if you break something once, you can break it again into even smaller pieces. People were glad there was no more Pope – but why have Henry's Church either? Some gave up God altogether – atheists. Some wanted to go to God direct, without any priests. All truth was in the Bible which they could read now it had been turned into English. Who needed more?

Thus came the PURITANS. They thought music, poetry and especially plays were SINFUL AND EVIL. Also, Puritans were often rich, as they worked hard, building up big businesses.

Watch out for them, Shakespeare. They could cause you a lot of bother.

So what did the Catholics do about it?
Not much. They waited for Henry to die. Then, when he did – wonderful. His first daughter, Mary Tudor, became Queen. She was still Catholic. The beheadings and burnings went on.

BUT NOW IT WAS THE OTHER WAY ROUND. Then Mary died. Elizabeth's turn.

Ah, Good Queen Bess! I bet she was really nice to everybody

Oh, no she wasn't. She could execute anyone she didn't like —they could be Catholics, atheists, traitors (otherwise known as "anyone she fell out with"). She could:

a) Hang them

b) Throw them in boiling water. Or oil

c) Press them to death between huge millstones

d) Hang, draw and quarter them

e) Burn them alive at the stake

f) Behead them (aristocrats only: they felt quite privileged)

Well, not her personally. But she knew some men who could.

31

Was that the lot?

Yes. Though when Guy Fawkes was sentenced to death in 1606 (Elizabeth was dead, but James carried on the good work) a special committee was set up to think of a REALLY AMUSING NEW WAY to kill him. But they couldn't, so they had to settle for boring old hanging, drawing and quartering after all.

Any more?

Isn't that enough? Shakespeare was setting off through a **very interesting country.**

Plagues, Plays and Puritans

So what sort of city did William come to?

Not a bit like London today, for a start. Instead of six
million people sprawled over miles and miles, there were
about 200,000 squashed in the square mile behind the old
Roman walls and a few suburbs beyond. If you went north
to Islington and Tottenham, you'd be deep in the
countryside. If you walked across old London Bridge
between its three floors of shops to the south bank you'd
come to Bankside and Southwark – and then nothing else
except wide, wild Kent and Surrey.

Inside the walls were narrow crisscrossing streets,
churches on nearly every corner, rows of shops, tall
timbered houses, great palaces, grimy hovels and a river

33

chock full of ships, with sails and masts nearly as high as the
spire of old St Paul's cathedral.

What about Queen Elizabeth?

She wasn't daft. She lived at Whitehall. This was outside
the walls.

What else was inside the walls?

A city council of merchants, craftsmen – and the dreaded PURITANS, giving Shakespeare and the actors a lot of bother.

Why did they give Shakespeare bother?

They thought plays were vain shows in which people forgot their duty to God and only thought about themselves. The theatre was a place of terrible sin which the Bible forbade. They really worried about the sins of their fellow men. And they had a lot to worry about.

Anything more?

Of course. Smell. Stink. Sewage running down the streets. Riots and murders. And above all:

PLAGUE.

Not just any old disease, but real, deadly, killer bubonic plague.

It started with nasty boils and finished with you being tipped into a big pit and covered with lime. It was brought by the fleas on rats which came to England in ships.

But didn't the council know what the cause was and do something about it?

Not really. The Puritan Council still thought plague came as a punishment for people's sins. Most sinful of all, of course, was the theatre. Not just sinful. TERRIBLE.

So they banned all theatres within the walls.

But if nobody dared go to plays, what was the point of Shakespeare coming all that way to act in them?

Who said they daren't go? They *loved* plays. Besides this Council only ruled *within* the walls. They couldn't stop what went on just outside. So that's where the theatres were, to the north, round Shoreditch and to the south, in Southwark. That's where the actors acted their plays.

All right, who were the actors?

They were the servants of aristocrats. If they didn't have the name of a lord, they were vagabonds and put in prison. Shakespeare was in Lord Derby's troupe. Later, Lord Derby was made Lord Chamberlain by Queen Elizabeth. So Shakespeare ended up with The Lord Chamberlain's Men. It sounded good. Nobody could touch them now, not even the puritans. So they thought.

What were the theatres like?

Small, made of wood and plaster with stages in the open air.
No lighting, so plays were put on in the afternoon. No
scenery: you used your imagination.

When Macbeth says,

"... Light thickens and the crow
Makes wing to the rooky wood.
Good things of day begin to droop and drowse
While night's black agents to their preys do rouse,"

the audience needed no dimmed lighting to imagine
the scene.

Sounds useless to me.

Not at all. That's why the words were so important. The plays were fast, with no pauses for scenes to be changed. Characters talked to themselves a lot.

That sounds mad. Were they?

Anything but. That's how we know who they are, what they think, what they feel. These soliloquies are the most memorable things in Shakespeare. Who do you think Hamlet thought was listening when he says:

"To be or not to be: that is the question..."?

Nobody. Except the audience, of course. (Though in this case, he was wrong. People were listening behind the curtains.

Afterwards, they decided Hamlet really must be mad. They were wrong too.)

Just thinking out Loud!

So did Shakespeare start writing straight away?

He would have acted first, and learnt what went on. He wasn't a bad actor – but he wasn't great, either. So he started writing plays – and soon learnt that trade as well. He got more and more popular. By the time he wrote *Richard III* and *Romeo and Juliet*, everyone knew he was *good*.

So everything was great now, was it?

Well, no, actually.

Poems, Patrons and more Plague

In 1593, the Plague came worse than ever. At last the Council got their way. They closed down all the theatres. The actors had to go out on the road again.

So there was poor William with no theatres in which to put his plays on and no actors to act them. What did he do?

Did he:

a) Say *"I'm fed up with this. I should never have come to London in the first place. I'm off home to Stratford."*

b) Say, *"I'm through with plays. I'll write stories instead and be a great novelist. Pity television isn't invented yet, I could have written for that. Or gone to Hollywood."*

c) Say, "I know, I'll just get a job like everyone else."

Well, what do you think?

Is it a)?

Sort of. He was definitely *very* fed up. And he did go back to Stratford a lot, to see his family, help them when things were hard and buy land and property to come back to one day in the future.

Is it b)?

No. There was no such thing as a novelist. Nobody wrote novels for nearly two hundred years. Besides, not many people could read. That's one reason why they loved plays. But if there *had* been TV – William Shakespeare would have been on the screen every night, writing scripts for *Eastenders, The Bill,* you name it.

Just think about it. Shakespeare wrote for money, nothing else. He'd have ended up writing Hollywod blockbusters.

Was it c)?

No it wasn't. Why not? I don't know. It just wasn't, that's all.

But surely he must have done something?

Yes, he did. He sat down and wrote a letter. It might have said something like this:

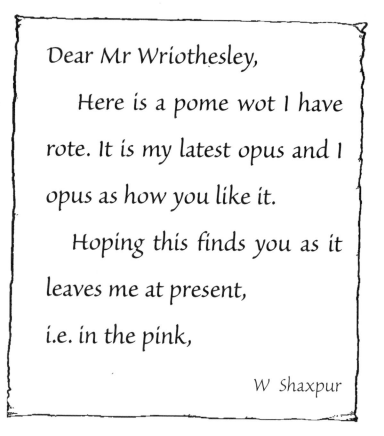

Dear Mr Wriothesley,

Here is a pome wot I have rote. It is my latest opus and I opus as how you like it.

Hoping this finds you as it leaves me at present,

i.e. in the pink,

W Shaxpur

This is **NOT** actually the letter that Shakespeare wrote. But it's what he meant.

Why did he do it? And who was Mr Wriothesley?

Shakespeare couldn't write novels, but he *could* write poetry. It was very popular with aristocrats, people round Queen Elizabeth's court, young lawyers and the like.

If Shakespeare wanted to make a living from writing today, he'd be paid by a publisher. Or he might get a grant to keep writing from the Arts Council. But not then. No, the way to do it was by getting a *patron.* Other poets did. So Shakespeare did too.

So what was a patron? A rich aristocrat who liked poetry, and especially poems dedicated to him. He might pay for a few more.

And Mr Wriothesley? Henry Wriothesley was only 19. But he was already the Earl of Southampton and as rich as they come. Queen Elizabeth thought the world of him. Ideal.

Or so Shakespeare thought. Sadly, in the end, he turned out to be the very worst choice Shakespeare could have made.

So William sent Henry a poem. Why should Henry be so pleased with it?

Because it was really rather a naughty piece of verse. It was a long story – *Venus and Adonis.* It was about this innocent young lad who is fancied by the Goddess of Love herself. He

ends up dead. She, being a goddess, doesn't.

Henry liked it. So William sent him another one – *The Rape of Lucrece* – in which Lucrece is fancied by ancient Romans.

Henry liked that too. So William sent him some sonnets. And then some more sonnets. And then even more. In the end he wrote 154 sonnets.

ONE HUNDRED AND FIFTY-FOUR. Yes, Shakespeare liked sonnets. So, it seemed, did Henry Wriothesley. Yes, sonnets were their bag all right. Sonnets were fantastic. Long live SONNETS.

Are there any questions so far? Ask me now, because I won't be stopping again.

Some Answers

Yes?
What is a sonnet?

A poem exactly fourteen lines long. They'd been going a long time and were very popular just then. Shakespeare liked them because he could pack a lot of meaning into a short space.

He could write lines which have never been forgotten:

Lilies that fester smell as rank as weeds

He could be regretful and melancholy, thinking of what used to be:

Bare ruined choirs where late the sweet birds sang

He could be mocking about some mysterious woman:

My mistress' eyes are nothing like the sun...

If hairs be wires, black wires grow on her head.

Who was she? Did she exist? No-one knows. No wonder she's called *"The Dark Lady of the Sonnets."*

Did Anne Hathaway know about this Dark Lady?

I don't know. But if she didn't exist, Anne wouldn't have worried too much. Don't ask me what she would have thought if the Lady was real. If black wires grew on her head, I doubt if Anne would have been too bothered.

Why couldn't Shakespeare spell his own name?

Nobody could spell their own names. Or anything else. Spellings kept changing all the time. They spelt words the way they sounded. It was printers who got fed up with this and insisted words were spelt the same all the time.

So who was this Robert Greene who hated Shakespeare that we met at the beginning?

He wrote plays. He had been to University and he had a lot of friends like Kit Marlowe, Thomas Kyd, John Lyly and George Peele who also wrote plays. They were called 'The University Wits'.

They thought that because they'd had such a great education they were the only ones who could write plays. They didn't think mere actors could possibly do anything like that.

But after Shakespeare and a few others like Ben Jonson started, plays were written by actors themselves, for their own companies. And, sadly for Robert Greene, the plays that William wrote before Greene died were loved by everyone. *William was top playwright!*

After the plague, the University Wits never wrote plays again. Greene was dead and Marlowe – who Shakespeare was friendly with and admired – was killed in a fight in a pub. An accident?

Never. It was a put-up job. Marlowe was a secret agent for the government.

So how did Shakespeare end up playing for Walsall?

I did say it was *much, much* later, didn't I? Craig Shakespeare was a midfield player for Walsall only a few years ago.

'Shakespeare' was once a common name in the midlands and is still around today. If William's only son Hamnet hadn't died in 1596 when he was only 10, there might have been more now.

Why wasn't Henry Wriothesley a good choice as a patron?

Wait and see.

Shakespeare in love – sort of...

Well, the plague went away. For a while, anyway. So the theatres could start up again. And on came the plays – play after play.

Think of them: *Romeo and Juliet, Richard II, Taming of the Shrew, Midsummer Night's Dream, Merchant of Venice.* And more besides. All completely different. All making people flock into Shoreditch and the theatre.

But Shakespeare **NEVER MADE UP A SINGLE STORY OF HIS OWN.**

What do you mean? Did he just copy the plays out?

No, definitely not. He found old stories from poems, ballads, legends, history books – and turned them into what he wanted. That was his great secret. He could take something old and forgotten and make it marvellous. Beside, he just didn't have time to think up new plots.

Ah, life on the stage. Fit to wear anybody out. Shakespeare was writing and acting and producing from dawn to dusk. He composed his plays very quickly – so that when he was dead, Ben Jonson wrote, *"He never blotted a line."* But Ben himself worked slowly and thought William would have done better if he had as well. So he added, *"Would he had blotted a thousand."* By "blotted", he meant "crossed out and altered." Cheeky devil.

Did Shakespeare never get any time off, then?

Yes, he did.

Did he have any friends?

Yes, he did.

Who were they?

There were mainly the other actors in his company –
Richard Burbage, John Heminges, Augustine Phillips and the
clowns Will Kemp and Robert Armin. And then there was
Ben Jonson.

Tell us about them

Burbage took all the big leading parts. He was Romeo,
Brutus in *Julius Caesar,* Hamlet, Macbeth, Othello, King Lear,
Antony, Prospero in *The Tempest.* As Burbage got older, so –
more or less – did the characters he played. He had red hair
and a terrible temper, so they say. Heminges
could do most things.

After William died, he and another
actor, Henry Condell, made sure all the
plays were printed. That's the only
reason we still know about them...

Augustine Phillips did the music for the plays.

Will Kemp was a great comedian. Once, he
danced from London to Norwich. Why? He must have been
sponsored. Or very fit. Or mad.

Robert Armin was very small and had long arms. He could tie himself up in knots. He was a *riot!*

Ben Jonson acted and also wrote plays. William acted in at least two – a funny one called *Every Man in his Humour* and a Roman tragedy called *Sejanus.* Ben used to be a bricklayer and William got him started in the theatre.

So were these theatre folk William's only friends?

Well...

Go on, tell us

Oh, all right. It's said that once he and Richard Burbage were after the same girl. Richard had arranged to see her one night and said she'd know who it was because he'd come as Richard III, the play he'd just been acting in. But when he knocked at the door and whispered,

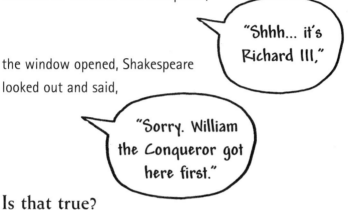

"Shhh... it's Richard III,"

the window opened, Shakespeare looked out and said,

"Sorry. William the Conqueror got here first."

Is that true?

If it is, DON'T TELL ANNE HATHAWAY.

Is there anything more you think you ought to tell us?

Not that I know of.

So Bill was a bit naughty when he was in London and miles away from Anne, was he?

Wouldn't you like to know! Wouldn't I, as well. Wouldn't everybody!

But I guess we never will.

Into the Globe

The century was nearly over. Things were going well for the Lord Chamberlain's Men.

Or were they?

Actually, they were in a mess. The theatre was nearly falling down. The man who owned the land was called Giles Allen. He was a puritan and deep down wanted the actors out. So he put the rent up so high they couldn't afford it.

So what did they do? Did they:

a) Break into Giles Allen's house while he was asleep, find the lease, alter it so it said *Rent – 5 pence a year,* forge his signature and break out again?

b) Say "Plays aren't worth all this aggro. Let's go and live in the country and commune with nature?"

c) Steal the theatre?

Well, a) might not have been a bad idea. They just can't have had anybody who could forge his signature.

People who were wise never did b) in those days. Unless they were lords with big estates. If they weren't they'd probably be peasants. For them, the country was hard and horrible. And nobody in his right mind would try communing with nature.

So they did c).

Don't be stupid. How can you steal a theatre?

Well, they did.

They had found some spare land on the south side of the river. The winter of 1598 was very cold. The Thames had frozen over. They chose a night when it was snowing hard, so nobody would be around to watch, their footprints would be hidden and they wouldn't be seen through the falling flakes. Then they took the theatre to pieces and loaded all the wooden beams on carts. A carpenter called Peter Streete

told them how to do it. Then they guided the horses and carts along the icy streets from Shoreditch to Southwark.

Did they take the carts across the frozen Thames?

Probably not or the theatre might have ended at the bottom of the river. More likely they led the horses across London Bridge.

Peter Streete rebuilt the theatre in 28 days. They called it The Globe.

It was – and still is – just about the most famous theatre in the world.

What did Giles Allen think when he woke up and found the theatre gone?

I should think he was furious. But there wasn't a lot he could do about it. He owned the land, not what was on it. Besides, who'd want to pull the Globe down, take it back to Shoreditch and put it up again?

No, once the flag was flying to show a play was on and

the audiences were streaming across the river, nobody would dare to touch the great Globe, most popular place in London.

"Sad stories about the death of kings."

Once there was a rather feeble king of England. He was kicked off his throne by the other nobles. This was nearly 200 years before William wrote his first play.

So what? – you may ask. Well, William wrote a play about him. Richard II. In it, King Richard says:

"For God's sake let us sit upon the ground
And tell sad stories of the death of kings."

This was not a very clever thing to say, because while he was telling stories, this man called Henry Bolingbroke was actually DOING THE BUSINESS. He had himself crowned, Richard locked up in a castle and then murdered.

People loved this play. All except Queen Elizabeth. She *hated* it. Surprise, surprise.

INTERRUPTION.

Very interesting, but you still haven't told us why Henry Wriothesley wasn't a good patron for Shakespeare to choose.

Your wait is over.

Henry W's best friend was the Earl of Essex. Once upon a time, Elizabeth rather fancied Essex – until she found he was plotting about who should succeed her. Guess who he had in mind. Why, Essex, of course.

To get rid of him Elizabeth put him in charge of an army sent to squash a rebellion in Ireland.

Essex asked Henry W to be second-in-command. Off they sailed.

THEY MADE A PIG'S EAR OF IT.

So they had to come back to England complete failures.

What did they do then? Did they:

a) Go to Elizabeth and say, *"We messed up. Sorry, Liz. But we've bought you a bottle of duty-free Irish whiskey and a bunch of shamrock to make up for it."*

b) Pretend they'd really won, make two soldiers dress up in green, kneel in front of her and say, *"Sure, Your Majesty, and aren't you the finest queen in the world, at all, at all, begorrah. Have a shillelagh."*

c) Realise there was no way out, start a rebellion, kick Elizabeth off the throne and let Essex be king instead.

No, it doesn't matter that myself, I'd try **a)**. They tried **c)**.

They laid their plans carefully.

Right. Put yourself in their position. You want to start a rebellion. What do you do?

Do you:

a) Get millions of people on your side with lots of

propaganda so everyone thinks you're right and rallies to your cause?

b) Recruit a huge army which can crush the ruling power with no trouble?

c) Plan a campaign which will carry you through the whole country and make the capital city and the government all yours?

d) Get some actors in a theatre to put on a play?

Myself, I'd do a), b) AND c). But Essex and Henry W, they thought they'd get away with just doing d). ...Mad.

So they went to Shakespeare's company and asked for a play to be put on specially the day before the rebellion was due to start.

Maybe this is what happened then.

SCENE:
THE GLOBE THEATRE

Shakespeare stands on the stage. He is thinking about writing a new play.

shakespeare

I know. I'll call it Hamlet. I wonder if I could nip across to Denmark and soak up a bit of atmosphere.

Enter Essex and Henry Wriothesley

henry w

I say, Bill, my old mate, how about putting on a play just to please a friend? A sort of request time?

shakespeare

Of course we will. Anything for you, Henry. How about 'Twelfth Night'? A few good laughs there. Or 'Romeo and Juliet'? Never a dry eye in the house.

essex

None of them. What we want is Richard II.

shakespeare

What, that old thing? We haven't done it for years. Wouldn't you rather have Henry V? Real patriotic stuff, that.

henry w
It's Richard II or the deal's off. But if you do
what we want when we want, we'll pay you 40
shillings extra.

shakespeare (amazed)
40 shillings?

essex
Yes, mate, 40 shillings. The time will come, give or
take a bit of inflation, when you won't get paid
that much for a Coronation Street script.

shakespeare
Well, if you put it like that, we might see our
way to...

essex (rather threateningly)
You'd better.

henry w (Taps finger on side of nose
Say no more, squire. Nudge, nudge, wink, wink,
know what I mean?

EXEUNT OMNES

Well, perhaps not quite like that. But Shakespeare's actors definitely did *Richard II* for the Earl of Essex the day before the rebellion for 40 shillings more than they usually got.

The day of the performance came. The theatre was packed. All went well. Then the Duke of York said: *"...plume plucked Richard.....his high sceptre yields/ To the possession of thy royal hand.../ And long live Henry, fourth of that name."*
Henry Bolingbroke answered: *"In God's name I'll ascend the royal throne."*

The audience started shouting, screaming and stamping their feet.

ESSEX

Ah, that's what I like to hear.

HENRY W

That Henry Bolingbroke knew what he was doing all right.

ESSEX'S SECOND BEST FRIEND, whoever he was

About time we had a proper king ourselves, not the stupid woman with too much make-up on that we've got now.

SHAKESPEARE

(mutters to other actors) Do you think we're doing the right thing here?

Well they very nearly weren't

Next day came the revolution. Did Essex and Henry win? No. What a shame for them that **a)**, **b)** and **c)** hadn't occurred to either Essex or Henry. Or Essex's second best friend. As a result, they didn't get very far. They were captured and brought before Elizabeth.

Elizabeth

I always knew Essex men were revolting. Take them away.

Where to? A big place by the river Thames with Beefeaters and ravens, beginning with **T.** Here Essex met a man holding something beginning with **A.** Soon, he lost something beginning with **H.**

What was it?

Well, he couldn't blow his nose. But it wasn't his handkerchief.

She took pity on Henry W and showed mercy. She put him in the Tower for life and took all his possessions away.

This is mercy? You could have fooled me,

He probably said as the jailer turned the key.

I have no idea what happened to Essex's second best friend.

So what about Shakespeare and the actors?

We were only obeying orders,

They said at Essex's trial.

They got away with it. The night before Essex was beheaded, they even acted a play especially for Elizabeth.

They knew which side their bread was buttered. In those days, you had to.

Any more questions?

Yes, there are.

You said Burbage was Romeo, Macbeth and Antony. So who played Juliet, Lady Macbeth and Cleopatra?

Well, they weren't women, for a start. Women were barred from acting. No, they were boys whose voices hadn't broken.

So that was how you started a career in the theatre?

Not necessarily. Shakespeare didn't. And a lot of boys ended up in all-boys' companies, run by St Paul's cathedral and the Chapel Royal. So everybody thought they were great – but they only became grown-up actors if they were too poor to do anything else.

They acted in the city, at Blackfriars, in the warm and dry in an indoor theatre, with lots of lighting and special effects. Shakespeare hated them!

You said at the beginning that William was taken to the Miracle Plays in Coventry. How can you possibly know that?

Well, I don't really. But it is a very good guess, and here's why.

There's a Coventry play in which King Herod appears and slaughters the Innocents to make sure Jesus is dead and can't be king. In it he gets very, very angry. The stage direction says:

> # Here, Herod rages on the pageant and in the street also.

So Herod was screaming his head off!

Back to *Hamlet.* Shakespeare's telling the players not to shriek and shout their words, because it *"Out-herods Herod." Convinced?*

No, not really. How do you know that?
Stick around and I'll tell you

It had better be more convincing than the last lot.
I'll do my best.

Feeling rotten

About the time he wrote *Hamlet*, Shakespeare does not seem to have been very happy. His plays are strange and gloomy. They are full of disgust – at himself and the rest of the world. He tries to write comedies, like *All's Well That Ends Well* and *Measure for Measure*. But where they're funny, they're also slightly sick and the characters are weird. He wrote his greatest play – *Hamlet* – at this time. It's a tragedy. But it's a lot more as well.

Hamlet is told by his father's ghost how he was poisoned by his brother Claudius, who then married Hamlet's mother, Gertrude. Hamlet vows revenge.

But he can't bring himself to do it. He has to work out a terrible problem in his mind. He drives his girlfriend, Ophelia, to suicide. When he does kill Claudius, it's a terrible mess. Hamlet ends up dead as well and so does nearly everyone else except his only friend Horatio and Fortinbras, Prince of Norway who leads in his army at the end. Perhaps an invasion is just as well. As Hamlet says:

"Something is rotten in the state of Denmark."

But what? And where, and how, do you find it? Was something rotten in the state of Shakespeare as well? Was something on his mind? Was it...

"Murder most foul?"

Perhaps something like this had just happened, when Shakespeare was buying New Place in Stratford.

SCENE:
THE OFFICE OF FLOGGIT AND GAZUMPEM, ELIZABETHAN ESTATE AGENTS IN STRATFORD.

Enter Shakespeare and Mr Floggit

FLOGGIT

So, William, you're interested in buying New Place. Very desirable property, if I may say so.

SHAKESPEARE

I've known it ever since I was a child. The nicest house in the town. I always hoped I might one day have enough money to buy it for my family.

FLOGGIT

So you don't worry about some of the things that happened in it.

SHAKESPEARE

I've been away a long time. You'll have to remind me.

FLOGGIT

Well, you couldn't remember the first one It was in 1563, the year before you were born. A William Bott lived there.

Nasty piece of work if ever there was one. He wanted all his rich son-in- law's possessions for himself. So do you know what he did?

SHAKESPEARE

No, but I can see you're going to tell me.

FLOGGIT

You're dead right, I am. First, this Bott forged some papers which said he'd get all his daughter's husband's possessions if she died without having children. Then guess what he did.

SHAKESPEARE

I'm afraid I'm getting a pretty good idea.

FLOGGIT

You're right. He poisoned his own daughter to get all the property.

Shakespeare does not answer, but starts thinking deeply

FLOGGIT

I haven't finished yet. The next to live there was another William, Underhill this time. He was poisoned as well. Do you know who by?

SHAKESPEARE

I don't think I want to.

FLOGGIT

By Fulk, his own son. That's who.

SHAKESPEARE *(to himself)*

A father murders his daughter, a son murders his father. What can be worse than murders within families? I'm not sure I want to buy this house after all.

FLOGGIT

Oh, don't take any notice of me. I'm always one for a joke. Just don't let it prey on your mind, that's all.

EXEUNT OMNES

Well, was it true? Yes, it seems certain that it was.

Was it knowing about these murders in his own house which made him so unhappy? Or was he feeling that way already and these murders merely made it worse? With all these murders inside families, Hamlet's Elsinore castle is like New Place must have been when Bott and the Underhills lived there.

Or perhaps there were things which went even deeper.

Such as?

Plague and bad harvests. Life was hard in England. Rebellion and riot were near. A friend of the Shakespeares, Richard Quiney, was elected as town bailiff. Sir Edward Greville, Lord of the Manor, didn't want him to be bailiff. So he sent his men to beat him up. They smashed him round the head with cudgels and killed him.

Nobody was ever punished for it.

"For who would bear the whips and scorns of time,
The oppressor's wrong, the proud man's contumely?"

says Hamlet. By "contumely," he meant "abuse" or "humiliation".

So very much was wrong – terrible things happening in Stratford while England was nearly starving

All except the rich. They were very rich. They'd got it, they flaunted it and they meant to keep it. Doesn't it sound familiar?

Besides, William was still grieving for his only son Hamnet not long dead. All his hopes now lay with his daughters, Judith and Susanna.

And what was happening in London? Was he having trouble with that mysterious Dark Lady of the Sonnets?

Who knows?

Goodbye Elizabeth – Hello James

If only Essex and Henry W could have held out for a couple of years. Elizabeth died in 1603.

Who was to succeed her? She left no children. England would be ruled by a stranger. This was terrible. Especially when they found out who.

King James. A Scotsman. Scotland was 'The old enemy'. Wars had been fought between England and Scotland and

there would be more yet. Scotland was a separate country
with its own king and James was already King James VI there.
Now he was to be King James I of England as well.

Worse. *He was the son of Mary Queen of Scots and
Elizabeth had had his mother's head cut off.*

It did not bode well.

But in the end, thing's weren't too bad. James seemed
to like the actors anyway. Soon Shakespeare's company

changed its name. Henceforth, they were to be **THE KING'S MEN.** So not everything in William's life was doom and gloom.

What could they do to show the king how pleased they were?

Why, act him a play, of course. So William wrote one specially.

MACBETH

The unlucky play.
Even today, actors won't call it by its name. So it's –

The Scottish Play

It's murderous.
Dark.
Flowing with blood.
Supernatural.

And, for James, very good listening. For while the witches tell Macbeth:
"Thou shalt be king hereafter"

they tell Banquo:
"Thou shalt get kings, though thou shalt be none."

When Macbeth has murdered King Duncan, who is a guest in his own castle, he knows he must get rid of Banquo. So he has him murdered. But Banquo comes to Macbeth's feast even though:

"...safe in a ditch he lies
With twenty trenched gashes on his head."

However, his son Fleance has got away and the accusing, mocking ghost marks the beginning of the end for Macbeth.

Yes, Shakespeare knew what he was doing. James was descended from Banquo and Fleance, so *Macbeth* is a play about when his family started being kings.

Clever old William. Never missed a trick if he could help it.

William's Last Years in London

Life at the Globe was as good as it would get for the King's Men.

But was it for Shakespeare?

King Lear is about an old man and his three daughters. Lear is king of England and divides his kingdom between them. But first they must tell him how much they love him. Goneril

and Regan say how wonderful he is. Great. But what does Cordelia, his favourite, say?

"Nothing, my Lord."
"Nothing will come of nothing. Speak again," says Lear.

But Cordelia repeats: she loves her father as much as a daughter should: no more, no less.

So start all Lear's troubles and the most harrowing tragedy of all that Shakespeare or anyone else ever wrote. The end is so painful that after Shakespeare died, nobody could bear to read it, act it or watch it. So the play was given a happy ending by someone else, which stayed until 1838.

But it's only a play. Why should Shakespeare be unhappy?

Was Shakespeare writing about himself, what he hoped for, what he feared? He had two daughters and he loved them. But did they love him? Did they worry him? Susanna was his favourite. But she was headstrong. However, when she married Dr John Hall, Shakespeare was very pleased. He really liked him. What about Judith? One day, she would upset her father very much. But perhaps not yet.

These terrible tragedies don't sound a barrel of laughs.

You're right. I wonder if this is what people thought?

"What's on today then?"

"King Lear. This old king gives his country away, dies and so does his favourite daughter. Lear's friend, the old duke of Gloucester, has his eyes gouged out. There's hardly anyone left at the end who's not dead. Do you fancy it?"

"What's the weather like?"

"Rain and wind. The Thames will be rough when we cross it. That thatched roof on the Globe will drip water all over me again."

"What do you say? Give it a miss?"

"OK. Let's hope it gets better for next week. It's Othello.

He's a big bloke who gets so jealous he puts a pillow over his wife's face and suffocates her."

"Charming. I bet we have to stand in the snow to watch that."

Yes, you had to be tough to watch Shakespeare's plays.

The King's Men probably thought the same about acting outdoors in winter. What could they do? Those rotten boys' companies had warm indoor theatres. Until they went broke. At once, the King's Men bought the Blackfriars Theatre.

And Shakespeare started writing completely different plays for it.

Romances. Fantasies. Lots of music, lots of spectacle, lots of lighting effects. They can have these now they're indoors. *Pericles, Cymbeline, A Winter's Tale.* And, above all – *The Tempest.*

Families are reunited. Lost children are found. But all's not well. There's trouble in them – King Leontes in *A Winter's Tale* is jealous and wants to kill his wife. In *The Tempest*, Caliban is a strange creature living on the island, who says to the magician Prospero:

*"You taught me language, and the consequence is
I know how to curse."*

Perhaps Shakespeare was tired of London and plays. Perhaps he wanted to look after his family more. Perhaps he'd made enough money. After *The Tempest*, in 1610 he left London and went back to Stratford. *"Our revels now are ended,"* says Prospero, and *The Tempest* ends with Prospero saying,

*"Now my charms are all o'erthrown,
And what strength I have's mine own."*

It's as if Shakespeare is saying, "I've written you all these plays over the years but now I'm tired and I'm just giving up."

That was it. Except for when they got him to help someone else, **NO MORE PLAYS FOR WILLIAM.**

The End

Didn't he get fed up, back in that dead-and-alive place?

It doesn't seem so. Besides, he kept going down to London to see how things were going. But he had a lot to do in Stratford. He had property to look after, a family to see off into the grown-up world, troubles all around as big to him here as anything in London.

And that was it, was it?

Not completely. He wrote part of *Henry VIII* with his friend John Fletcher. He helped in a play called *Cardenio*, now lost.

A missing play by Shakespeare? Why can't someone find it?

Wouldn't they love to! It would be beyond any price now.

What did he do in London when he went there?

In 1613 he bought a house there, near the Blackfriars Theatre. But in the same year – DISASTER!

Go on. What was it?

The roof of the Globe should never have been thatched. The King's Men were playing *Henry VIII*, a cannon was fired on stage and a spark caught the straw.

End of the Globe, a pile of ash.

'ere... do you feel hot?

That cannon's deafened me... It's a quarter to four.

So what did the King's Men do?

Built another Globe Theatre at once. This time, the roof was tiled.

And William helped, of course.

No. It seems he didn't. He saw the smoking heap, said, *"Enough is enough"*, sold his theatre shares and got out quick.

Was he sad?

Who can tell. He had enough to do at home anyway. Judith was seeing a lot of Thomas Quiney. Compared with his father, who was murdered by the Lord of the Manor's men, Thomas was useless and *a rat*. But nothing could be done to stop it – in 1515 they were married.

Why was he useless?

Because everything he tried went wrong. He tried selling wine and messed it up. He tried selling tobacco and lost money. He needed money badly and tried very hard to get it off Shakespeare.

Why was he a rat?

Because after he and Judith were married, he went around with other women.

What did Shakespeare think of this?

What do you think? When he made his will, he left things to Judith

> "and any such husband as she may have".

So he wouldn't accept that Thomas was married to her! Even when the lawyer nearly wrote

> "son-in-law,"

it's crossed out and

> "My daughter Judith"

written over it. So much for Thomas.

And to his wife Anne went

> "My second-best bed with all the furniture."

Generous or what?

Who got most in the will?

Susanna, his favourite daughter.

Why was he making a will?

Because it was March 1616 and he was ill.

What was the matter with him?

Some say Ben Jonson and another actor turned up to see him, they all went out drinking and William got so drunk he took a fever or had a stroke.

Some even say Thomas Quiney, because William wouldn't help him, murdered him by giving him poison.

But what's most likely is this. That stream flowing past New Place was very unhealthy and there wasn't much in the way of loos and clean running water in 1616. Shakespeare caught typhoid fever and once you got that, you just had to wait until it killed you.

So on April 23rd, 1616, the same day as he was probably born 52 years before, he died.

But his story had hardly started.

So what have we got?

What do you mean, his story had hardly started?

When he died all those years ago, what do you think his last words were?

Were they:

a) "Why do you keep on staring at me, Thomas?"

b) "Pen and paper, quick! I've just thought of a brilliant new play. It's going to be the best thing I've ever done."

c) "I do hope they choose me to be 'Man of the Millenium'."

I haven't a clue.

Neither have I. But I do know they weren't **c)**. He never thought he was going to be famous. He believed he was just someone who'd earned good money writing plays for his company.

But now – all over the world his plays are acted, in every language, in every style, All the time they end up saying *more* to us, *more* and *more* and *MORE*. He's the biggest draw for tourists any country can ever have had. He's driven kids at

school mad because everyone has to read him. Some think it's boring.

But it's not. It's wonderful. Why?

That would need another ten books!

titles in the series